What is young?

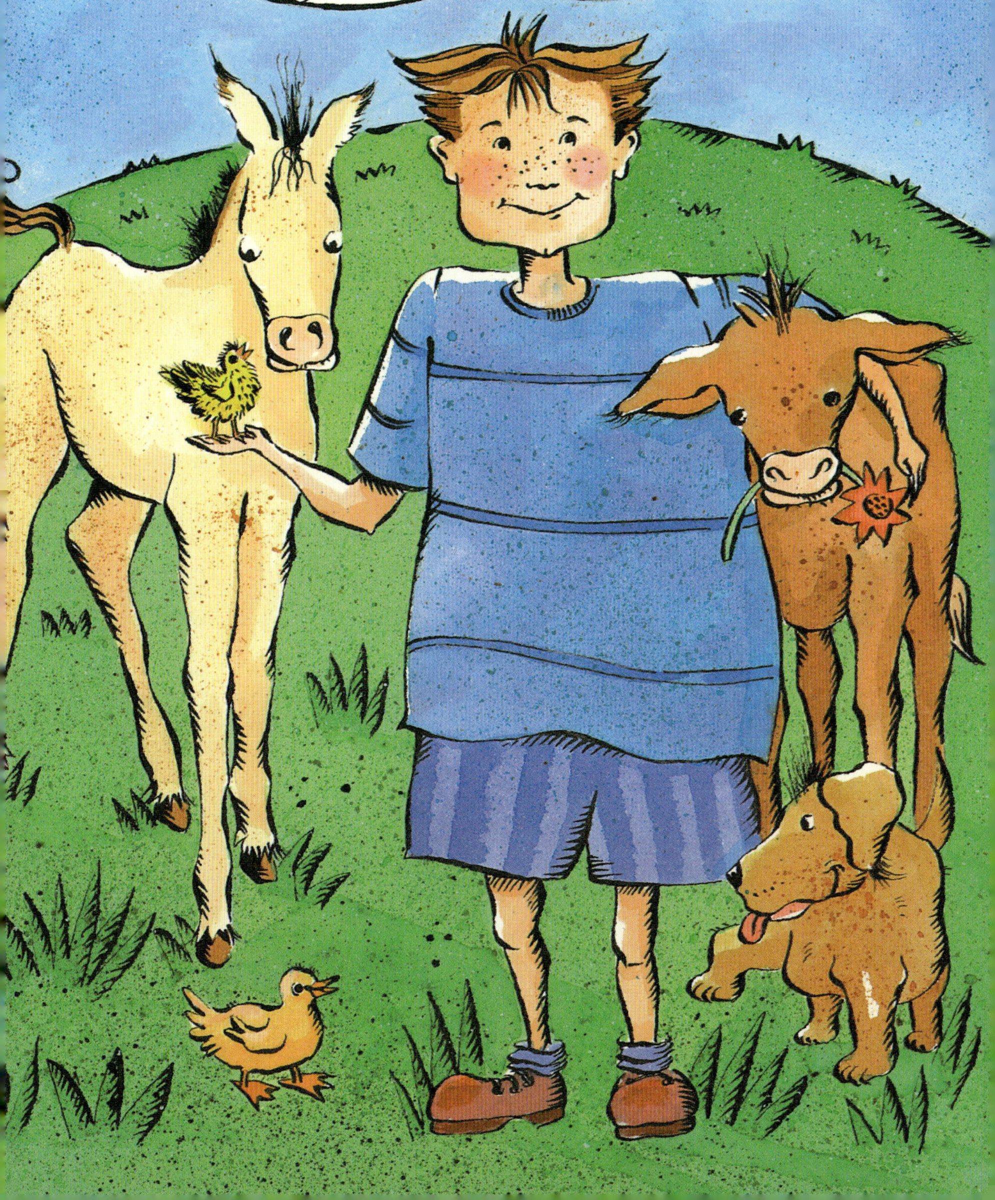

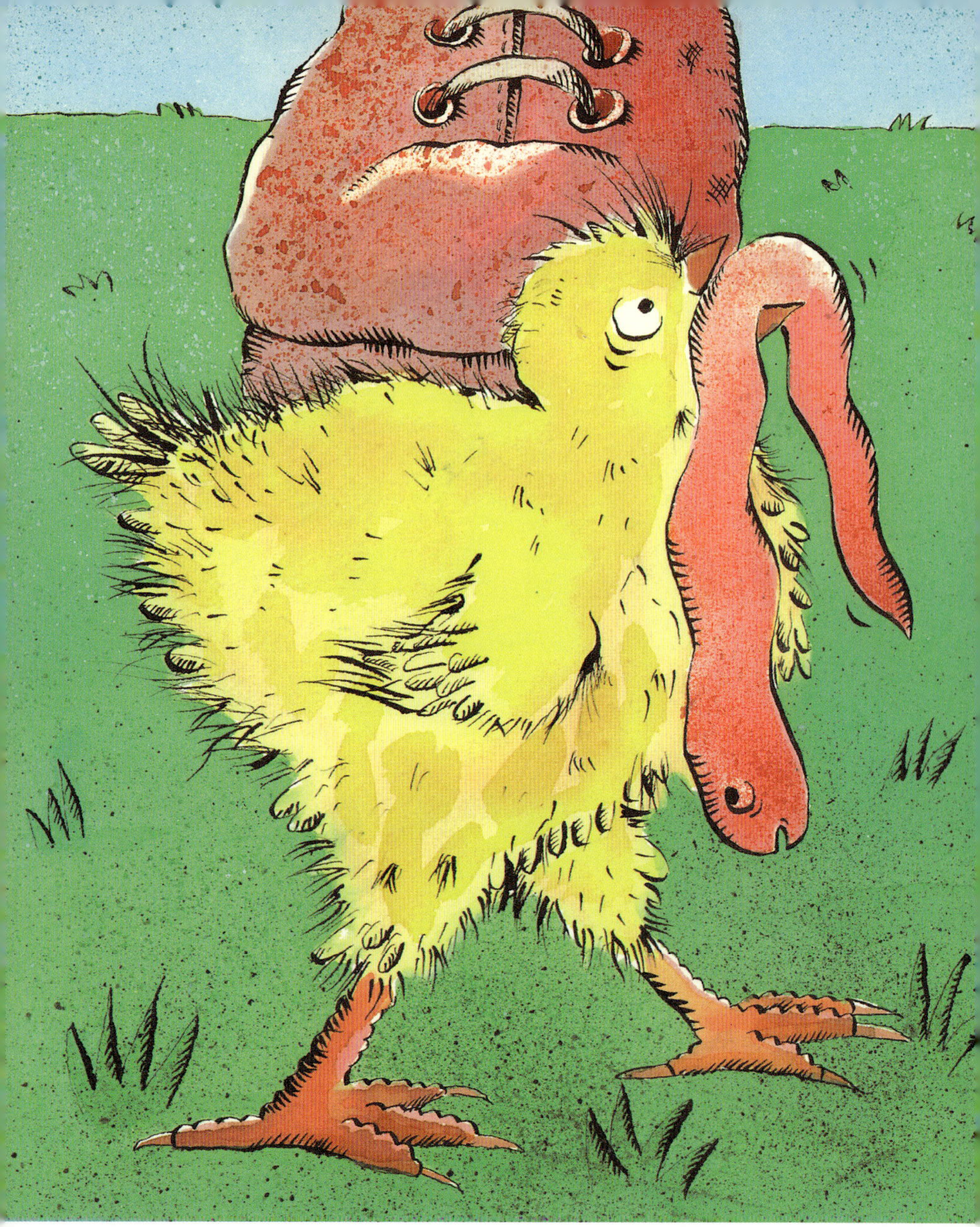

A chicken is young.

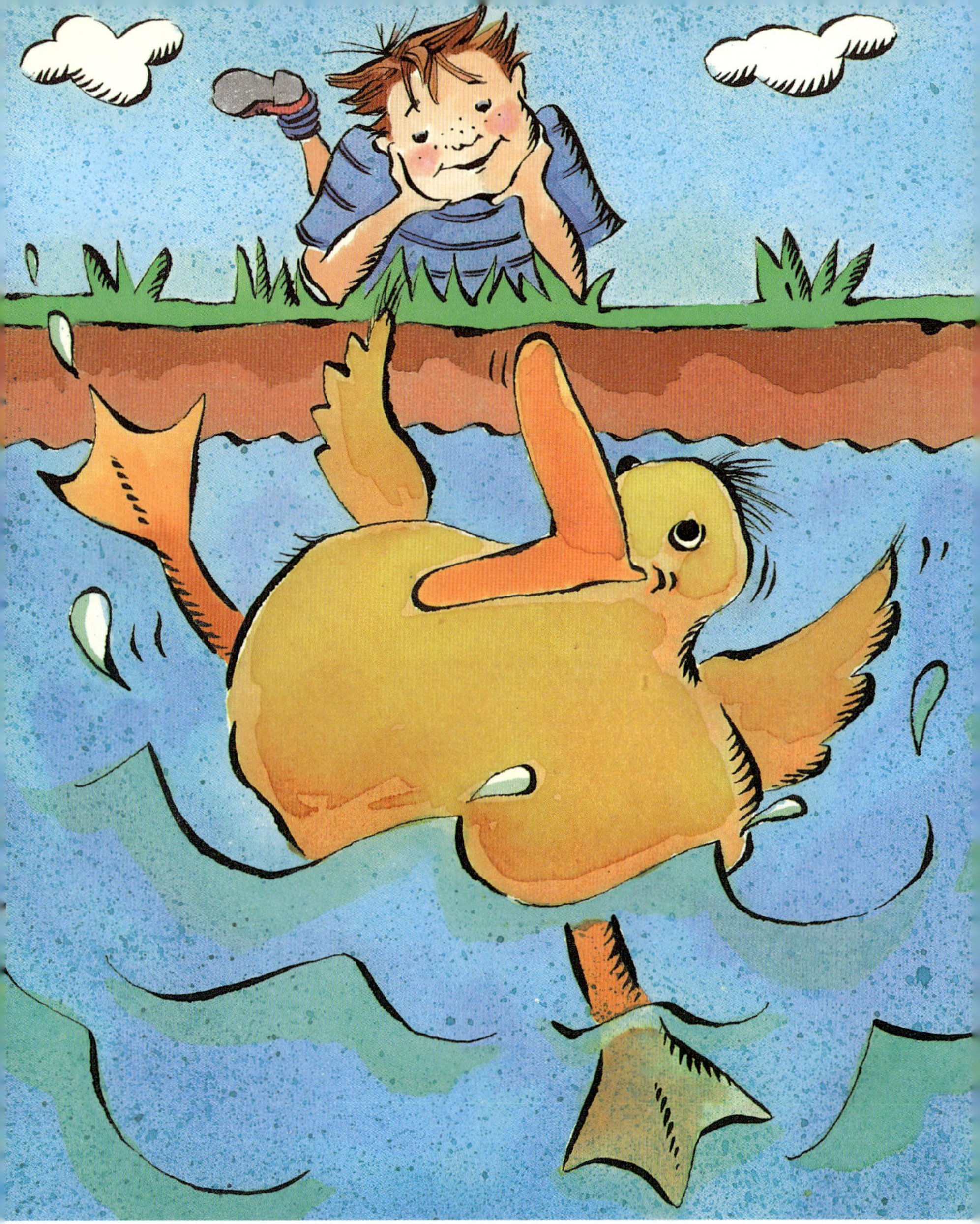

A duckling is young.

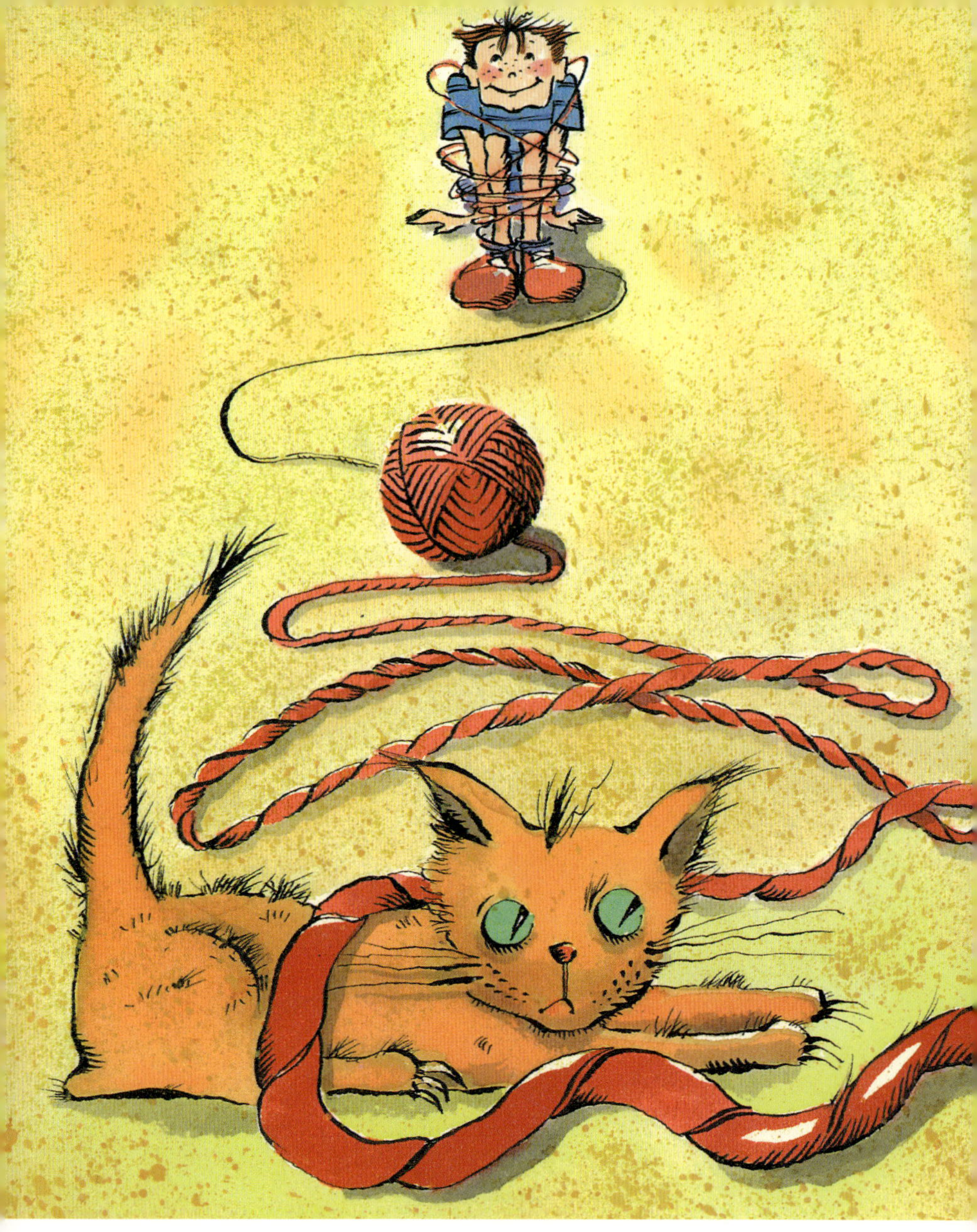

A kitten is young.

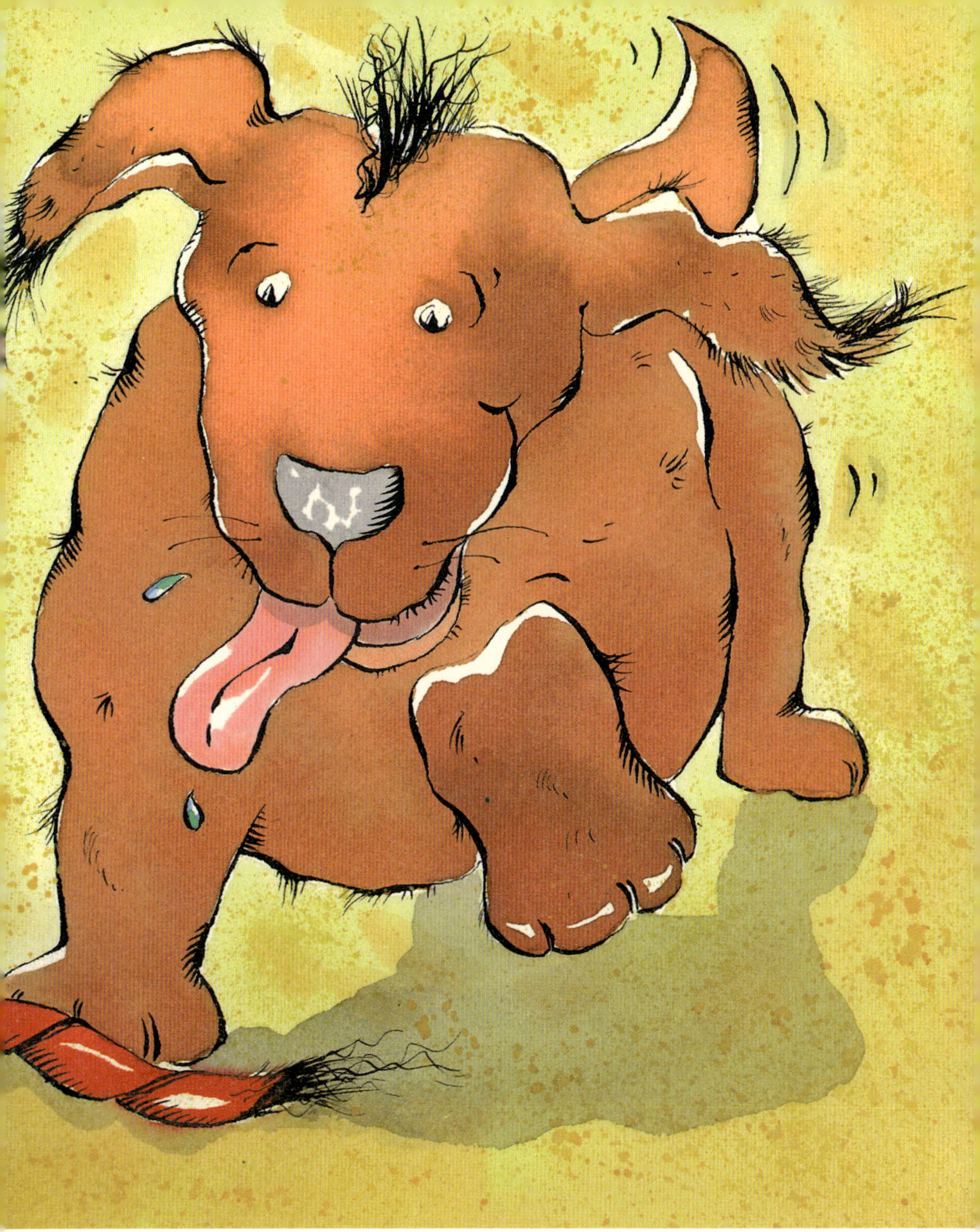

A puppy is young.

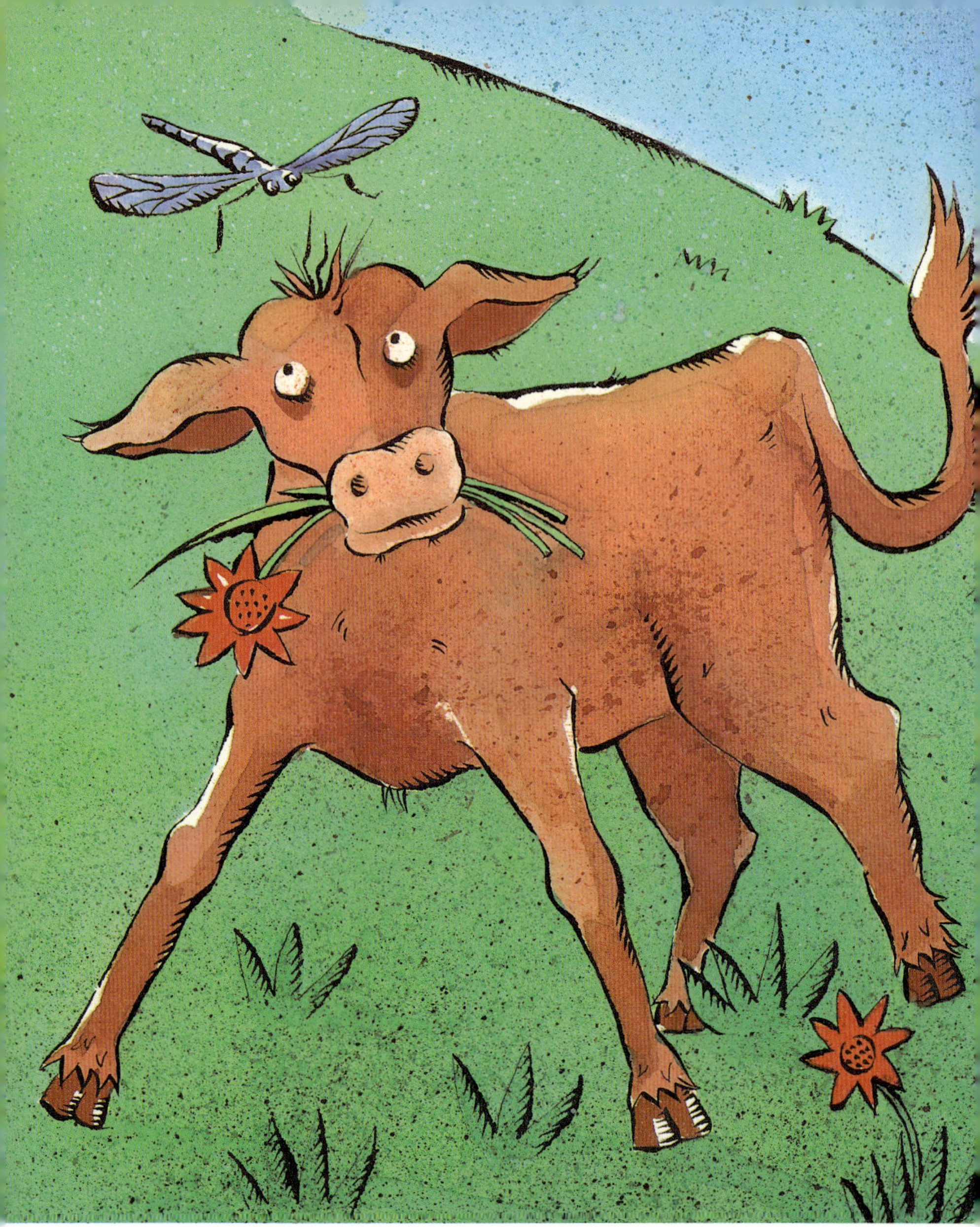

A calf is young.

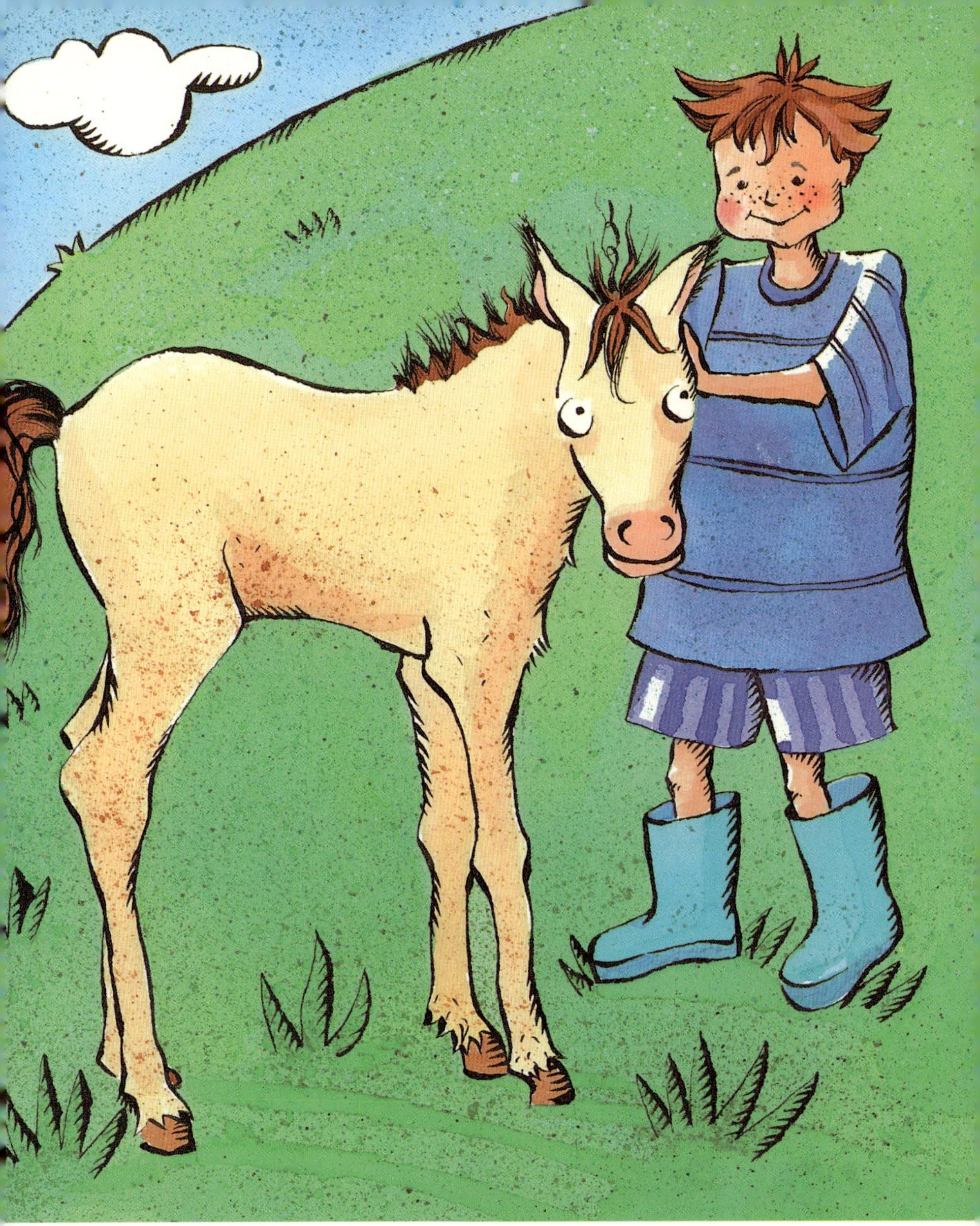

A foal is young.

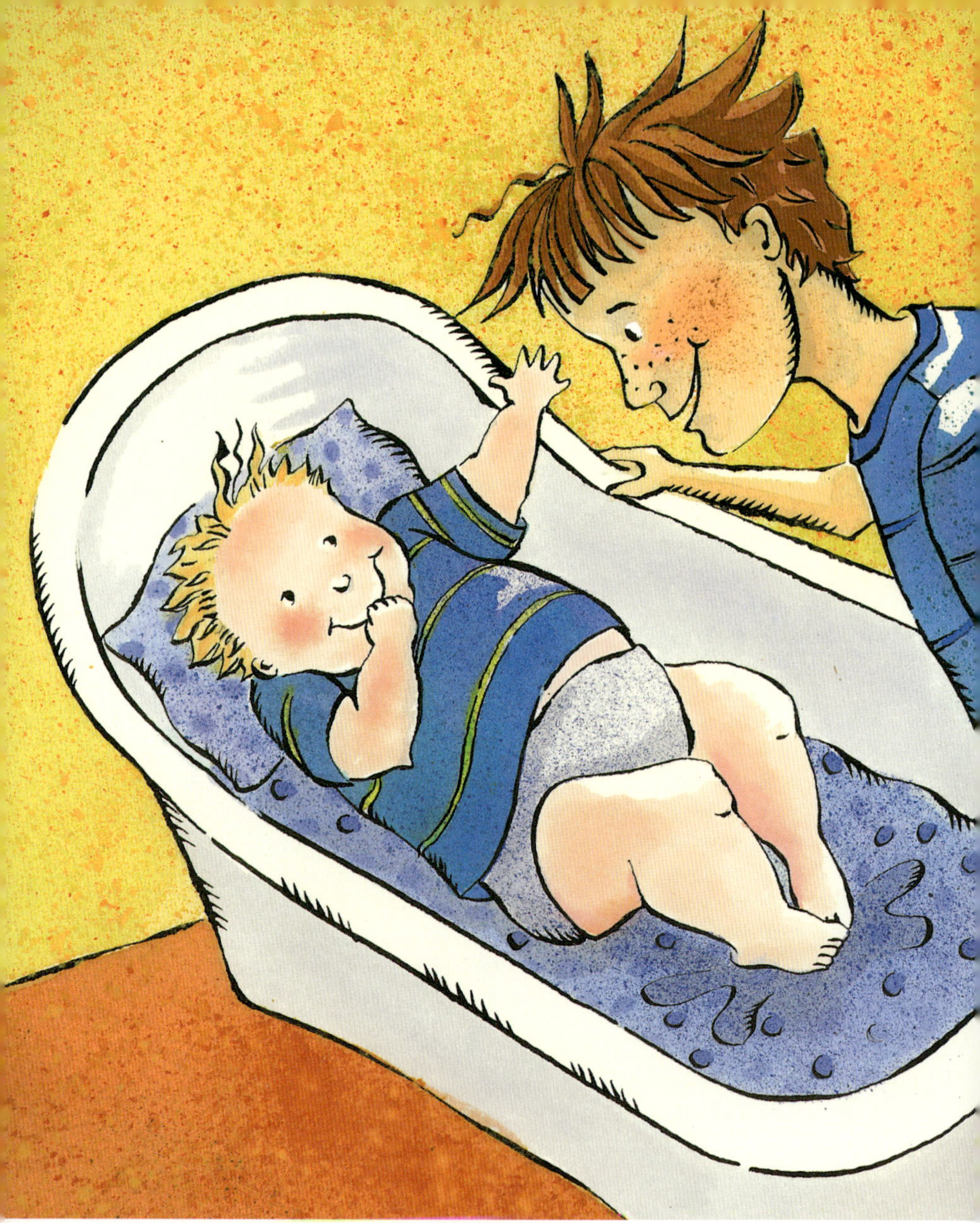

And my baby brother is *very* young!